Fireplace Styles

FIREPLACE STYLES

FORM, FUNCTION, AND DESIGN

ALISON DE CASTELLA

COURAGE BOOKS

AN IMPRINT OF RUNNING PRESS
PHILADELPHIA • LONDON

2003 Salamander Books Ltd
Published by Salamander Books Ltd.
The Chrysalis Building, Bramley Road
London W10 6SP, United Kingdom

© Salamander Books Ltd. 2003

A member of **Chrysalis** Books plc

This edition published in the United States in 2003 by Courage Books, an imprint of
Running Press Book Publishers
125 South Twenty-second Street
Philadelphia, PA 19103-4399

9 8 7 6 5 4 3 2 1
Digit on the right indicates the number of this printing

Library of Congress Control Number: 2002117088

ISBN 0-7624-1626-2

Notice: The information contained in this book is true and complete to the best of our
knowledge. All recommendations are made without any guarantee on the part of the
author or publisher. The author and publisher disclaim all liability in connection with the
use of this information.

CREDITS

Commissioning editor: Marie Clayton
Designer: Cara Hamilton
Reproduction: Anorax Imaging Ltd
Printed and bound in China

This book may be ordered by mail from the publisher.
But try your bookstore first!

Visit us on the web!
www.runningpress.com

Contents

Introduction

From the distant past, the fireplace has been the center of people's existence. Over the centuries it has progressed from being a utilitarian necessity into both a technical tour-de-force and a style icon. At first it was there to give warmth, and to provide a cooking hearth. As it evolved, and houses expanded to have multiple rooms, the need to use it for heating water and food in the main living area became less important. This change of function has been reflected in fireplace design over the years, and each period in history has developed one or more quite distinct styles. Decoration came to the fore, and the heat and pleasure taken from gathering around a handsome—and sometimes awe-inspiring fireplace—became a delight and source of contentment. The status bestowed on houses by their beautiful and ornate fireplaces was enormous. Concealed inside many such houses are some of the most secret of hidden treasures. Here we try to uncover some of them for your pleasure.

This book tells the story of the evolution of the fireplace, right though from early Mediaeval times to the present day. It includes many stunning photographs of elegant, beautiful and sometimes astonishingly over elaborate fireplaces. The text gives a glimpse into the background behind the design and creation of many of the major pieces, and information on some of the well-known designers and architects who influenced how fireplace styles changed over the years.

Left: *A elegant open fire grate, with its decorated cast iron fire back beautifully framed by the marble fire surround. The painting above completes a Classically-proportioned and aesthetically pleasing picture.*

Early Styles

In early buildings, the fire was in the center
of the room and the smoke drifted out
through any opening. The modern day
fireplace originates from early Norman times.

Above: *A copy of an imposing Tudor-inspired chimneypiece with
ornate, carved stone overmantel.*

Opposite page: *An early fifteenth century chimneypiece, probably
originally from Leeds Priory, but now situated in a private residence.*

In the early evolution of the fireplace—from the primitive wood or peat fire lit on a slab of stone during the Saxon times through to the Mediaeval period when the fireplace evolved into a considerably more efficient edifice—the most important room was the common hall.

The Saxon dwelling, whether it was a palace, a manor house or a lowly one-room cottage, was built around the fireplace. Rooms could be added on at different stages of the life of the house, but the fireplace was the hub of early English domestic life, providing heat to cook food, boil water and warm the inhabitants. The common hall was usually on the ground floor, and was open to the roof. The fire would be placed in the center of the room and the smoke would drift out through open windows, crevices in the eaves—or sometimes through a hole in the roof created for this purpose. There is a line in the "Nonne Preestes Tale" in *The Canterbury Tales* by Chaucer that goes "Full sooty was her bower and eek hir halle, in which she eet ful many a sclendre meal." This evocatively brings home the likely sensation of living in a building that did not have a large enough hall to disperse the smoke! Coal was less objectionable than wood when burnt in close quarters like this, but the residents would have had to sleep around the fire at night to keep warm, so even when using coal life must have been very uncomfortable. Recessed fireplaces with chimneys were installed as early as the twelfth century in other rooms in the house, but even though the central fireplace was such an important part of domestic life, chimneys did not come into general use in the central hall until the early sixteenth century. Smoke turrets or louvers were introduced during the reign of Henry III according to written records, although there are no examples still in existence. Initially they were built solely for the purpose of assisting the smoke out of the building, but gradually the chimney stack evolved as a highly decorative architectural ornament.

A rare example of a central early hearth can be found in the great halls at Penshurst Place in Kent. There is a pair of andirons in situ—albeit from a slightly later date—that are placed exactly as the originals would have stood in the fourteenth century. Occasionally a brazier that would burn peat or charcoal would be used, instead of a log fire. It would have been an iron dish raised on legs, and these were used up until the end of the seventeenth century.

The modern day fireplace originates from the early Norman times. Unlike the single story Saxon dwelling, the Norman household was frequently set out over two stories and therefore could not accommodate the Saxon method of allowing the smoke to drift out through the rafters. Early chimneypieces were large, slightly cambered hoods, supported on stone jambs or corbels. The recesses of the capacious fireplace could contain niches in the back wall, where a clay pipe or cup could be placed. There would, in some households, be sufficient room to hang cuts of meat so that they could be smoke-cured.

By the start of the Tudor and Jacobean periods, the fireplace had evolved from a huge overhanging stone hood, sometimes even supported by columns, to a more discreet affair. There was sufficient area around

Opposite page: An unusual early example of a fire hood inside the chimneypiece itself, which was to reduce smoke in the room. This one dates back to the early 1500s, and probably came from Leeds Priory.

Below: One of only a few remaining Elizabethan fireplaces. The frieze above would have carried the crest of the family home.

the fire to allow a number of people to huddle close to the warmth, and occasionally a settle or bench would be set into the fireplace for comfort. The lintel was generally a single heavy beam and the opening of the fireplace was usually wide and rectangular to permit sufficient draught to oxygenate the flames.

Sometimes the kitchen fireplace even had an ingenious system of shelving installed on each side of the hearth—the shelves were narrow and ran from back to front of the fireplace and were used for baking loaves. Special flat shovels called "peles" were needed to retrieve loaves placed at the back of the oven. A surprisingly small number of these ovens have been discovered, so it can only be assumed that bread was so cheap to buy that the time and labor cost of producing loaves at home could not be justified.

Meat provided a much larger proportion of the Mediaeval diet than it does in the twenty-first century. Roasting spits were used for cooking it—an age old method that originated in Norman times. The meat

Above: This kitchen fireplace dates back to the early sixteenth century, when the room it is situated in would have been the kitchen. The wooden lintel and the stone fireback are made from local materials available at the time. The crude workmanship reflects the rural setting of this piece.

would be taken up to the table and served directly off the spit, hence the spit would often be made of silver. New types of spit and turning mechanisms were gradually brought into play, although it was not until the second half of the sixteenth century that clockwork or draught-operated devices started to catch on, in an early attempt to cut down time-wasting chores. There was even a small breed of dog known as a "turnspit," which had been specially trained to operate the spits by walking on a wheel or drum fixed high on the wall near the fireplace. The treadmill was attached to the spit by a spindle. It was not a happy profession for a small animal, particularly if he was turning the spit for a large joint of meat to feed guests at an inn—a task taking many hours. Indeed if the turnspit happened to spot the chef going to the larder to fetch a raw cut of meat it would make itself scarce, leaving the hungry guests to sit down to a slightly more vegetarian meal! Dogs continued to be used until the early part of the nineteenth century, when oven-cooked meat became the norm.

Hampton Court Palace in England has many examples of the Tudor fireplace—particularly within Wolsey's kitchens, where one can see examples and appreciate the massive scale of these cooking areas. Sloping brickwork partitions were built into the fireplace, dividing the cooking area into sections and allowing several different rungs of notched irons to be built in to support the spits. The extremely over-heated kitchen "knaves" could therefore turn many pieces of

Right: *A typical cross-corner Tudor fireplace with a heavily engraved mantel, situated in the King's Room, Hampton Court, England*

Below: *An early fifteenth century chimneypiece with a carved stone surround and brick jambs. This is a fine example of how the fire would have been used with all the cooking utensils stored within the fireplace.*

meat or chickens simultaneously, thus satisfying the well-documented gluttonous appetites of Henry VIII, his courtiers and minions during the feast days.

Other items that were in use to tend, contain or decorate the fireplace during this period were:

Andiron: a word of unknown origin, but probably a corrupted version of the old French "andier," with "iron"—the material from which they were made—attached, and confusing the whole with brand-iron. Andirons were used to hold up the burning logs, as well as to support the spit. Early andirons could have a cresset crowning the tall "stauke," so that a cup or candle could be placed there for convenience—although they were not necessarily designed with this purpose in mind.

Creepers: these were small stands that lifted the smaller pieces of wood.

Firedog: this name did not come into use until the Elizabethan period. One can see how the term was derived as the firedog did have a slightly canine look, with two squat front legs, and a tall and often decorated stauke, which could be topped with anything from a simple knob to an ornate crown that representing the head. The body of the dog was the billet-bar—the bar supporting the logs (known as billets) and this ended in a balancing stand. Firedogs became more and more decorative as the English gentry became aware of the Renaissance Italian arts movement during the Tudor period. Firedogs could be cast or wrought iron, and brass decorations could be incorporated. During the Elizabethan period ornate silver scrolls and rosettes were added and the whole item became a glittering affair, reflecting the brilliance of the flames.

Curfew: this word derives from the French "couvre-feu" (cover fire). It was originally just an earthenware dish, but it later developed into a brass or copper hood to place over the flames to make the fire safe for the night. It would have a small handle on the top, and it was often decorated with detailed symmetrical patterns or scroll-work.

Fireback: this item came into play during the fifteenth century. It was an iron plate set at the back of the fireplace, to protect the brick from over-heating. These pieces again evolved into highly ornate decorative features within the fireplace. The early models were

Above: *A typical chimneypiece design of a Tudor times. The heavily carved overmantel would often depict religious figures or a family crest.*

Opposite page: *This fireplace shows a different mix of designs— Classical, Heraldic and Traditional—all being used together.*

made using sand molds, pressing pieces of carved wood into the sand to create the raised patterns. The molten iron was poured into the depressions in the sand and this produced bas-relief designs. There was a huge scope for variety and innovation in these pieces. They changed from the wide rectangular plates that fitted the huge early Tudor and Jacobean fireplaces to narrow and tall plates with shaped tops—sometimes curved or scrolled dependant upon the design.

Early Tudor fireplaces were quite simple and unadorned, a practical installation with no decorative appeal other than an occasional simple rope detail around the surround. There is strong evidence of this because Cardinal Wolsey, who was a man who liked to surround himself with luxury and grandeur had very plain fireplaces within his apartments. Towards the middle of the 16th century, not only were the fireplace accoutrements becoming more ornate, but so were the surrounds and overmantels. There are many surviving examples of ornamental carving and applied decorations around the country. They often show the disjointed nature of fireplace design around this time, as odd snatches of information from Renaissance Italy were taken out of context by noblemen competing to flaunt their wealth and status. These were applied to the fireplace at will, often mixing design styles— Classical, Heraldic and traditional—in one piece.

Most of the decorative and complex wrought and cast iron pieces used in the Tudor household would have been produced in and around Brede, on the Sussex-Kent border in England. There is still evidence of this industry when you drive through the area, as you come across the many place names such as "Hammer Ponds," "Furnace Farms," "Forge Cottages," and so forth. The ancient oak forests of the Weald supplied the required quantities of charcoal that was used to smelt the iron. However, as the oak ran out, smelters started experimenting with coal and eventually switched to the coal entirely, which forced the industry to move elsewhere.

As fireplace designs became more interesting, so they steadily became the focal point of the room. Carved Tudor roses, nudes, gilded scrolls and heraldic shields were added above the overmantel, leading the eye right up to the cornice. Longleat in Wiltshire, England, contains an impressive later example of the carved fireplace, which incorporates columns, foliage, nude embracing figures bearing fruit on their heads, a

clock, a compass, arches, a cornice and is topped with an oil painting. This was installed around 1575–80, but even this was not as extravagant as some fireplaces that were being designed during this period.

The famous chimneys of Hampton Court Palace are in typical Tudor brickwork style from the early sixteenth century. Although they have been renewed since the originals were built, they appear to have been faithfully copied. The chimneys were individually detailed, either using the bricks decoratively, or carving the column of the chimney and then placing them in groups of contrasting styles. Again the average craftsman had only a vague understanding of Classical design from Italy, so often peculiar-looking chimney stacks emerged, sometimes representing columns but supporting nothing. Robert Smythson was an architect who designed a number of these peculiar hybrid

Below: *A copy of an early piece that has taken its design inspiration from a number of sources, such as Tudor, Elizabethan and very early Gothic. The carved stone overmantel depicts religious artifacts.*

chimneypieces c. 1560–88—examples of his work can be seen at Wollaton Hall in Nottinghamshire, and Burghley House in Northamptonshire, England.

Cleaning the complicated passageways of early chimneys was always a potential problem, but small boys were used right from the start. Sometimes the chimneys were stepped—and occasionally iron bars were set into the sides—to create steps for these boys to climb.

Generally there is very little consistency in fireplace, fireplace utensil or chimney design during the transitional period of the early sixteenth century. Gothic, Classical Italian, Heraldic and French styles were all experimented with by different architects. The design often fought with the practical aspects of the fireplace, and with the materials available in the region. The fireplace even had an influence on furniture design to an extent. In order to cut down the freezing draughts that must have chilled the back of the person seeking warmth at the fireside, the high-backed settle evolved.

During the Elizabethan period, fireplace design became much more intricate and detailed. There was a lot of money about that had been made available through Henry VIII's dissolution of the monasteries. This had been distributed amongst his coterie of favorites, and they started trying to outdo each other in terms of the grandeur and magnificence of their houses. There is a fireplace at Loseley House in Surrey, England, which is carved out of a single huge piece of chalk—a local material from the nearby chalk downs. The craftsmen has used an effect known as "vermiculated rustication," which creates the type of detail found on a frilly iced wedding cake. Although the design of this particular fireplace is late Elizabethan in style, it is believed that—together with some other features in the house—it was taken from Henry VIII's Nonsuch Palace, and could therefore have been made around 1540.

The hearth itself had now reduced in size, because the fireplace had become more efficient at emitting heat. There was no longer any need for the inhabitants to huddle about the flames, sitting within the fireplace recess in order to remain warm. This gave more scope to designers who wished to decorate the overmantel and the sides of the fireplace. Sometimes the grander rooms would have paneling, which incorporated the fireplace with harmonious carved surrounds to unify the features of the room. There is a very beautiful and richly-carved example of a late Elizabethan style fireplace at Burton Agnes Hall in Yorkshire. This fireplace, which dates from c.1601–1610, depicts bas relief figures going about their daily lives—doing such things as weaving, washing or dancing—with a spreading tree supporting a heavenly array of nudes dancing above. Capping this scene is a cornice, which in turn supports decoration of an entirely different style, c.1570, that has been taken from another house. This contains heraldic shields and statues, and has a pediment containing a crowning heraldic shield. The whole edifice is an imposing two stories high.

Although there was no definitive Elizabethan style—because there were still so many influences and extravagances incorporated—the one thing that did change almost unanimously throughout England during the Elizabethan Renaissance was the move away from Gothic style. This was largely due to Henry VIII, and the massive upheavals that he caused within the religious sector, which halted building works for a period long enough to lose the skills of a generation of Gothic masons.

Up until the early seventeenth century, fireplaces were largely designed separately from the buildings and consequently one would often find jarring and strange details such as a Classical overmantel within a Gothic hall. Inigo Jones adopted a very different and holistic approach of designing the fireplace and chimney within the overall scheme of the building—thus giving birth to modern day architecture.

Useful dates:

Henry III	1216	Henry VIII	1509
Edward I	1272	Edward VI	1547
Edward II	1307	Mary I	1553
Edward III	1327	Elizabeth I	1558
Richard II	1377	James I	1603
Henry IV	1399	Charles I	1625
Henry V	1413	Commonwealth	1649
Henry VI	1422	Charles II	1660
Edward IV	1461	James II	1685
Edward V	1483	William III &	
Richard III	1483	Mary II	1689
Henry VII	1485	Anne	1702

French Classical Style

The most elegant period
in history.

Above: *An ornately-carved wood fireplace, with gilt mirror above. This type of design was initiated and greatly favored by Christopher Wren.*

Opposite page: *This Italian-inspired fireplace uses an unusual green malachite— which is found in the Urals—and was built for the Yusupov family of Russia.*

Inigo Jones was a major influence on the development of style, as both an architect and designer, in both the late seventeenth century and into the early eighteenth. As people traveled through Europe on the "Grand Tour" the ideas being brought back to their home countries were both varied and diverse. Because influence from Italy and France were paramount, Jones was able to unify the vast array of ideas, making them coherent and turning them into beautiful creations. After returning from his own trip to Italy in 1614, Jones felt the lack of experienced craftsmen to implement his designs. He set about teaching workmen—who previously had produced good but not spectacular work. His perseverance in educating these workmen greatly benefited the artists to follow. Christopher Wren, for one, was eternally grateful for the work Jones did before him in training artisans into a new ways of thinking and working.

In his Italian sketch book in 1615 Jones commented "In all inventions of capricious ornaments one must first design the ground, or the thing, plain, as it is for use, and on that vary it, adorn it. Compose it with decorum according to the order it is of…" He deplores the overuse of capricious ornamentation on the façades of the houses he designed, but in his thoughts for chimneypieces, or the inner parts of a house, these detailed and ornate decorations were deemed necessary to be used. Despite the early hindrance of a lack of qualified workers in the type of designs he wanted to produce, Jones left some of the most ornate, beautiful and memorable chimneypieces that exist today. The heritage he left has been revisited many times over by artists in the course of history, and there are plentiful examples reproduced in grand homes across America.

Fine examples of the elaborate and ornate style of grand chimneypiece can be seen in houses like the Marble House, Newport, which was built in 1972 for the Vanderbilt family. The finest example can be seen in the Ballroom; the elaborate centerpiece of an extravagant room is the flamboyant chimneypiece. The figurines

Opposite page: This ornately carved chimneypiece is a very fine example of the kind of work copied from designs by Inigo Jones. The heritage he left has been revisited by many artists and has inspired many examples that can be seen today in grand homes across America.

supporting the mantelpiece are carved from black marble, and they depict youth and old age. They support an overmantle showing the mask of Dionysus, surrounded by heavily carved scrolls, which is a masterpiece of decorative art and stunning workmanship. This spectacular piece is gilded, as is most of the decoration of the ornamental Ballroom, and was made by J. Allard et Fils of Paris, which later became known as Alovoine et Cie. The house itself was designed by Richard Morris Hunt for the Vanderbilts, as their country cottage, and it was based on the Petit Trianon at Versailles in France. The whole building shows an excess and flamboyance of design befitting the extravagant lifestyle of such a well-renowned family. It was finished in time for the coming out party in August 1892.

In England, Inigo Jones achieved the highest architectural position possible at that time, being appointed surveyor-general to Charles I, where upon he was put in charge of the building of the Queen's house at Greenwich. Because of Jones's background in fine art and his early training as an artist, many aspects of his creativity came through in his liking for the theatrical in his pieces. He was known for many styles of fireplace, and the marble overmantels he instigated became a fashion, which continued into the eighteenth century. Not many great architects were working at this time, and copies of the few really good ones abounded. Repetition of the basic design was frequent, and the details of the carving or decoration were often left to the craftsmen working on the piece—and since many of these traveled across the country to wherever work was required, it is possible to find designs reproduced again and again. The ornately-carved marble pieces were often the focal point of the room, reaching up to the ceiling. They encompassed every style imaginable, incorporating figures, dramatic drapes and swags, Classical columns and heavily carved pediments—many were truly spectacular. Famous amongst his many well-known pieces are the chimneys in Wilton House, Salisbury, England. Two of these, completed in 1652, are known as the "Cube Room Fireplaces." The Cube rooms—one single and the other a double—were named because one is a perfect cube and the other is exactly a double cube. They were built for the Earls of Pembroke by Jones and his nephew John Webb, and

were of an incomparable beauty in their time. The double cube room fireplace, which was specially designed to incorporate a van Dyke painting, consisted of a spectacular carved overmantel, with gilded and colored escutcheons surmounting the whole piece. The center painting by Dick van Dyke is of the children of Charles I. The over-elaborate scrolls, drapery, cresting and inlaid marbles, together with the statues of Peace and Plenty and Corinthian columns, makes this fireplace monumental in its overall beauty and scale.

Jones produced many chimneypieces for this house, and although all were ornately festooned and gilded, none were comparable to the Cube Rooms, However, all show the significance of the work of this great master. Jones was not renowned for his domestic work—he was best remembered for the churches he produced—but what does remain shows not only his skill as an artist and designer, but also the skills of the master masons and carvers who worked for him.

One master carver who is best identified with Jones is Grinling Gibbons. His work epitomizes Jones's influence on the styles of this time, but Gibbons became known in his own right as such a master of his trade that he was commissioned to work on many important houses of the time, including Hampton Court Palace near London, England.

By the latter part of the seventeenth century, and after Inigo Jones's death in 1652, a transitional period began. The influence of the French can be seen much more, and fireplace design was again being dictated by architects, following the style of popular architecture. Many of the new styles were indeed different to what had gone before and for a period the characteristic Louis XV scrolls and curved lines—often carved in a dark, heavily-veined marble—became popular. This was a style that many craftsmen copied in America, and it is still very popular in homes across the continent today. Many examples can still seen, with historic

houses showing some of the finest pieces. Beautiful sweeps and curves are associated with this style, and these are shown to best advantage with a simple overmantle of a gilded mirror.

However, this soon when out of fashion as Christopher Wren became the next major influence on fireplace design. He was able to utilize the training Jones had already given the master craftsmen, whose skills had improved and now were comparable to the standards of the French and Netherlands workers. A complex mix of tastes—both continental and English—soon began to become apparent. Wren very much had his own technique, and the Queen Anne style became synonymous with his name.

Wren had a liking for simpler styles, and one of the chief characteristics of his fireplaces was the use of heavy bolection molding in stone or marble around the fire surround.

As a general rule, Wren rarely placed the mantelshelf at the ordinary height and the overmantels blended together with the paneling of the rooms. Although they were still aesthetically pleasing, they were not the dominating chimneypieces that had been

Opposite page: The flamboyant chimneypiece in the Marble House Ballroom, Newport. Built for the Vanderbilt family, it depicts the figures of youth and old age carved in marble either side of the fireplace.

Right: The over-elaborate scrolls, drapery, cresting and inlaid marbles, together with the statues of Peace and Plenty and ornate columns, make this fireplace monumental in its overall beauty and scale.

produced by previous architects such as Holbein and Jones. Wren also had a great liking for the placement of the chimneypiece across the corner of the room, as seen in his work in Hampton Court Palace and the Queen's House in Greenwich—which he subsequently improved after Wren's initial designs. John Evelyn was very critical of this practice of asymmetric room layout—he felt it took away the formality of great rooms, and made it difficult for people to gather round a fire in the traditional way.

When he was made Director of Royal Building, Wren became a very important figure in the architectural world of England. He was commissioned by King William & Queen Mary to design a new palace at Hampton Court to replace the old Tudor one. Work began in 1689 on a suite of rooms and galleries, which surround what is now referred to as the Fountain Court. It is here in these Staterooms that a selection of the best of Wren's work can be seen.

In the King's Drawing Room, a fireplace of beautiful simplicity still exists. The fireplace its self has stone sidings with a simple molded design. The fireback is made of cast iron and shows rampant andirons, and is completed with a simple white marble hearth. It is above, in the raised mantel and full height overmantel, that all the ornamentation exists—heavily carved wainscot oak, festooned with cherubs, wreaths and flowers by the master carver Grinling Gibbons, and surrounding a portrait of Isabella, Archduchess of Austria. It all makes what at first appears a simplistic style into a very beautiful chimneypiece. Grinling Gibbons was first discovered by John Everlyn in 1671 and was brought to the attention of Charles II and Sir Christopher Wren, under whose patronage he flourished. Many architects used the artistry of Gibbons—he was even known for carving a very fine point-lace cravat for

Opposite page: Wren frequently used mirrors in his designs, to allow the dandies of the day to admire themselves. This piece, with its heavily gilded mirror, is a fine example of the variety of styles that can be seen in the many private homes and grand houses that were built around this time.

Below: This ornately carved fireplace, with its gilt overmantel mirror, was built in 1852 in one of the Yusupov Palaces in St Petersburg, Russia.

the Duke of Devonshire out of lime wood. His genius was renowned and many pieces have been attributed to him—even though it would have been impossible for him to have created all the carving himself! His trademark was an open pea pod, and any carving with this hidden within it is guaranteed to have been carved by Gibbons.

Wren was a frequent user of mirrors in his designs, to allow the dandies of the day to admire themselves. Fine examples of these styles can be seen in the Queen Mary Gallery in Kensington Palace. One in particular has an overmantel in the form of a mirrored window, with the curtains carved from wood. In the same palace, in the King's gallery, Wren produced a most unusual chimneypiece. It consists of a circular dial, decorated with a map of the north-west of Europe, which has a central pointer connected to a rod controlled by the weather vane on the roof above, to show the direction of the wind outside. This device was a most ingenious way to amuse the aristocracy of the time, and showed how mechanical a brain Wren possessed.

A simple desire for change was the only reason that many of these styles were finally supplanted. Copies of the French style of Louis XIV became very popular for a while, before giving way in their turn to the extravagances of Chippendale—especially his chinquarai chimneypieces.

During the course of the seventeenth century fireplaces became the norm in the bedchambers—although they were never used if the person sleeping there became sick—so it was commonplace for the value of a house to be dictated by the number of chimneys it had. It was therefore a great status symbol to have numerous chimneystacks—so much so that a tax of two shilling for each hearth was brought in. It yielded $300,000 a year—a phenomenal sum at the time, but it was extremely unpopular with the poorer households. When William III came to the throne he abolished the tax, after it had only been in force for a little over 25 years.

Most large houses were relatively unscathed by this taxation and we have to be thankful—or the most beautiful examples could have been lost to us forever.

Right: *The French style of Louis XIV became very popular for a while, before giving way to the extravagances of Chippendale.*

Georgian Style

The Georgian era was one of elegance
and refinement, and the fireplace
became part of the architectural
concept of the room.

Above: *Fireplaces in this period often incorporated classical features in their design, either in cast marble or stucco panels.*

Opposite page: *Later Georgian fireplaces show a stylish simplicity, without the heavy carving and over-elaborate designs or earlier periods.*

With the advent of the eighteenth century, elegance and refinement came to the fore. The style of architecture known as Georgian was developed in England during the reigns of George I (1714–27) and George II (1727–60) and it evolved into something that was much simpler and more classic than the lush baroque look of the seventeenth century. Georgian style was based on Palladian designs, after a sumptuous book translation of I *quattro libri dell'architettura*, by the celebrated sixteenth century Italian architect Andrea Palladio was published in installments in 1715. Palladian style, although simple, was very grand since it was based on the Roman and Renaissance buildings seen in Palladio's native Italy.

Although Georgian style began in England, it quickly spread across the world. This was partly because of England's strong trading links at the time, which meant wealthy English merchants settled in different countries—and of course wanted the same style for their houses that was fashionable back home. Also England, being the head of an Empire, had a style to aspire to. One of the best known exponents of Georgian architecture in America was Charles Bulfinch, who had visited London during his Grand Tour through Europe.

American craftsmen also used the same style books produced for their counterparts in England during this period, so naturally American styles automatically developed very much in tandem with English ones.

In the early eighteenth century, there was no standardization of parts or designs, so there were as many designs of fireplaces as there were people with individual tastes. The "design book" chimneypieces seen at that time were often rococo in style—following the excesses of the previous century—with an ornate overmantle which many considered to be overblown and out of proportion for these houses. James Gibbs, in his Rules for drawing the several parts of architecture published in 1732, gives six patterns of chimneypieces with ornate panels above. Three of the designs have frames over them adorned with pediments, often

Right: *The Palladian-style fireplace, although simple, had a very grand origin since it was based on the Roman and Renaissance buildings seen in Palladio's native Italy. The expanding world and international travel meant American fireplace styles automatically developed very much in tandem with the English ones.*

broken: "they have the same proportions, as to their openings, as those in the former plates, but these are far more ornamental."

Isaac Ware was another exponent of heavily decorated pieces, in his Complete Book of Architecture, written in 1756, he says, "A principal compartment should be raised over it to receive a picture. This will be very happily terminated by a pediment possibly broken to receive a bust, a shield or other decoration." Examples of his elaborate fireplaces can be found in such stately homes as Castle Howard and Sudbrooke Park in England.

Socially, a new middle class was now emerging, with the substance and means to acquire extravagant houses, built in the style of the great architects. These extravagant houses, built in the styles of the great architects, became known as "copybook" houses, the design being taken from the architectural books of the

Opposite page: *"A principal compartment should be raised over the fireplace to receive a picture. This will be very happily terminated by a pediment possibly broken to receive a bust, a shield or other decoration."*

Below: *A fine example of an arched pediment as detailed in* The Rules for drawing the Seven parts of Architecture *by James Gibbs.*

Bottom: *A heavily-carved and ornate fireplace, which shows a design more popular in the early part of this century.*

great seventeenth century architects such as Christopher Wren and Inigo Jones.

As the Georgian style developed and came into its own, Chippendale, Ince and Mayhew's rococo or chinoiserie designed chimneypieces became fashionable, although no true Palladian architect would ever have contemplated using them. Although these designs are separated by only twenty years from the very heavy and elaborate pieces of Gibbs, they heralded a new lightheartedness not seen before. With Chippendale becoming popular through his published designs, styles—and peoples' perception of them—started to change dramatically. A new look began to emerge—stylish simplicity, with the emphasis centering on a lighter touch, and without the heavy carving and over-elaborate designs that can be seen in the Grinling Gibbons-influenced carved chimneypieces produced by Wren. One of the most admired architects of the time, William Kent, was a favorite designer for the "tabernacle form," which was composed of columns, entablature and pediments. Often split, the pediment would tower above the opening for the fire, which appeared small in comparison. Kent's designs were always grand, his treatments bold and massive in proportion, but what should be remembered is that they were designed for houses that were monumental in scale.

By way of contrast with the palace grandeur, the smaller houses built during the century adopted a simpler variation of the bolder style. The overmantle became architectural in feel, with a mirror panel or painting above, supported on either side by large volutes and often with a triangular pediment above. Architects paid careful attention to the selection of materials used and the designs of their fireplaces. The more ornate and elaborate designs were used in the state rooms and simpler styles and materials were kept for the private areas of the house not normally seen by guests. The ram's head was a favorite form of enrichment applied to the consoles—or overmantels as they later became known.

Adams heralded a sweeping change in the overall look of the chimneypiece. He made it part of the architectural concept of the room, rather than a dominant feature unrelated to the interior design. This became the style of the day in the latter part of the

Above: This kind of detail was known as "copybook;" often the designs were taken from the architectural books of the time and reproduced.

Opposite page: A fireplace of stylish simplicity, with the emphasis centering on a lighter touch, and without the heavy carving and over-elaborate designs seen previously in the earlier part of the century.

eighteenth century, and was immensely popular. Whereas previously the fireplace had overpowered the room in which it was placed, Adams designed the whole room with the fireplace integral to the space in which it stood, thus creating a harmony with the repetition of a single motif within the room. His preferred material for his most spectacular pieces was a statuary white marble from the Carrara quarry in Italy. In its pure white form it was very rare, so the importance and status of a room could often be recognized by the quality of the marble chosen for the fireplace. Adams would often inlay different marbles within the chimneypiece. Panels created along both upright columns and the mantel were filled with marble or composite—yellow sienna and verde-antique were among his favorites. A fluted detail with a color infill was also to be seen in his designs. The use of columns, either in pairs or double pairs, seemed to be another trademark use of classical features incorporated by Adams into his designs. Often the columns were finished with an Ionic capital and enhanced by a contrasting marble, or, for a less important room, painted stucco was often used.

By 1778 fine ceramic cameos came into fashion, notably those of Josiah Wedgwood who produced designs by Flaxman. Intricate, contrasting friezes were created by skilled craftsmen, following Adams' classical designs. He made free use of flowers, acanthus leaves, scrolls, ribbons and ram's heads, while sphinxes, urns and vases were also subjects for decoration, his style being Greek rather than Roman. The designs for chimneypieces were elaborate and even more elegant.

What singled Adams' designs out from others of the time was their good proportions, symmetry, grace and lightness—they were always aesthetically pleasing. The use of stucco panels above the mantelshelf depicting scenes of the Greek classics was another characteristic

Below: An excellent example of the kind of Classical features incorporated by Adams into his designs. This fireplace shows the columns finished with an Ionic capital and enhanced by a contrasting marble, together with typically delicate wrought iron details on the inner surround and fire screen. The simplicity of this design carries a grace and elegance that was synonymous with Adam's fireplaces.

Above: *Another example of an Adams-inspired fireplace. The applied gilt decoration adds emphasis to a Classical design.*

Left: *A detail showing the corner of an Adams fireplace. He had a great love of figures and urns and they are seen often incorporated into his designs, alongside the delicately-carved swags he also favored.*

of Adams designs—they were seen in the most elegant of homes, and many were very elaborate in design but always had a delicacy of form.

Many original examples of exquisitely beautiful Adams fireplaces still exist today Osterley Park on the outskirts of London, for instance, is a magnificent fusion of his styles, showing Adams and his many designs of chimneypieces to their full advantage. This building was begun in 1761, and since Adam took nineteen years to complete the work it illustrates his changing style as he matured. The early styles in the Library, Hall, Eating Room and Drawing Room show bold but not heavy decoration, often using the same motif in the frieze, bookcase and chimneypiece. In the Drawing Room, this motif is even carried through onto the apron of the grates to produce an accord within the room. As Adams progressed in his middle years, he refined his designs even further—and in his anxiety to avoid heaviness the designs became much more linear and intricately minute in scale, creating a delicacy and refinement not known previously.

While Adams was designing chimneypieces of exquisite beauty, his brother, John Adams joined a famous iron founder, the Carron Company of Stirlingshire. Together they were responsible for creating a new look in fire grates. Dog grates had become more fashionable than the cumbersome iron baskets that had been used previously, and the Adams brothers brought in a new form giving them a line, balance and proportion that enhanced the complete design of the chimneypiece. Seated on their slender legs, the dog grates were polished to a high sheen that resembled precious metal, the casting was fretted and woven like black lace and the design flowed in graceful lines—these became known as jewel grates. An original jewel grate stands today in the Victoria & Albert Museum. It was constructed with two fronts—a winter front and a detachable summer front—both beautifully constructed. The summer front is fixed by a spring attachment, which was easy to remove. Copied throughout the world, many of these grates are still in use today. Osterley Park Drawing Room is an interesting example of Adams' willingness to experiment with different metals. The dog grate here consisted of

a mixed metal called "paktong," which was an alloy of zinc, copper and nickel that together had a yellow tinge. He felt they created a harmony, within a room of the different elements.

Whilst architects were concentrating on the design of the chimneypiece, scientists were more concerned with making the fireplace more efficient and economical. A great deal is owed to Count Rumford, who in 1798 first published information to fulfil the interest that was taken in the working of the fireplace as a whole—although his ideas were not brought into general use until the next century.

Below: *Floral swags were another characteristic of Adams designs. They were seen in the most elegant of homes, and many were very elaborate in design—although they always carried a delicacy of form not seen before.*

Opposite page: *Adams also favored the use of stucco panels above the mantelshelf, often depicting scenes from the Greek classics.*

American Colonial Style

A style developed in America, but with its
roots in Europe and Scandinavia.

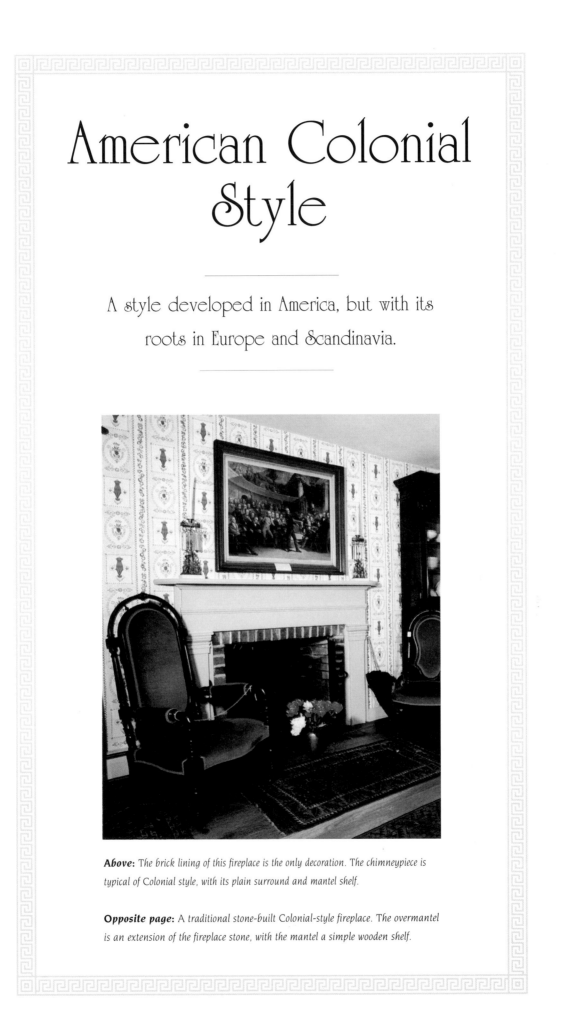

Above: The brick lining of this fireplace is the only decoration. The chimneypiece is
typical of Colonial style, with its plain surround and mantel shelf.

Opposite page: A traditional stone-built Colonial-style fireplace. The overmantel
is an extension of the fireplace stone, with the mantel a simple wooden shelf.

The American Colonial style has its roots in Europe and Scandinavia—immigrants from these areas brought the decorative palettes and construction methods from their homelands when they arrived in their new country. These were modified by the materials available, and by the styles already current in America. "Colonial," in fact, covers several quite diverse styles, depending on the area of America in which it developed. One distinct style, for instance, is that developed in New England. Here, the harsh climate conditions and the plentiful supply of timber from local forests led to houses that were based on the old timber-framed buildings of northern Europe, with clapboard sidings, wattle-and-daub interior walls and whitewashed interiors. In the southwest, there were more Spanish influences, so the style is based on Renaissance and Baroque elements. Another major facet was the English Georgian style, elements of which were incorporated from the late seventeenth century.

Early Colonial style tends to be very simple, as people were more concerned with shelter than aesthetics. Inside, the basic ranch-style chimneypiece incorporated all that was required for cooking and heating a large room. It was basic in its design and very functional. This style has carried on today, and is often seen in relatively modern homes—of course the need to cook on the fire has been eliminated, but the general design has remained the same. A huge beam of wood above the fire opening, often raw-cut direct from the tree, forms the mantel from which utensils—and later decorative items—would be hung. The open grate is large and dominates the room—in earlier days this would also have had the mechanics to hold cooking pots and spits for meat. Later, when the kitchen was moved into other rooms and cooking was done away from the large fireplace, these items were left for decoration. A fine example of this type of Colonial fireplace can be seen in Fair Lane, in Dearborn, Michigan, home of car manufacturer Henry Ford. In this house the Field Room—which was the hunting room—has a fireplace with a traditional wood beam mantel,

Left: *In the home of car manufacturer Henry Ford, the Field Room has a fireplace with a traditional wooden beam mantel, upon which an inscription has been carved. The quote from Thoreau reads "Chop your own wood and it will warm you twice."*

upon which an inscription has been carved. The quote from Thoreau reads "Chop your own wood and it will warm you twice." Beneath it is a massive, stone-clad fire surround, with a brick center. This form of Colonial style chimneypiece is quite often seen today and it is beautiful in its simplicity and structure. Often a style adopted for cabins and hunting lodges, it suits isolated surroundings very well.

Another very good early example of American Colonial can be seen in a log cabin built in 1931 at

Opposite page: This is a reconstruction of the home in which Abraham Lincoln grew up. The early nineteenth-century, rural fireplace that has been installed has a basic rough-hewn wood mantel, with the stone being used for the fire back, lintel and jambs.

Below: A more traditional working kitchen fireplace, which incorporates some Colonial elements, can be seen in Adena, home of a former Governor of Ohio. It has a small range on which to cook, with hanging storage above.

Knob Creek, Kentucky. This is a reconstruction of the home in which Abraham Lincoln grew up. The early nineteenth century rural fireplace that has been installed also shows a basic rough-hewn wood mantel, with the stone being used for the fire back, lintel and jambs. Roughcast bricks are used for the hearth—all these materials are elements synonymous with this homely and functional style. This particular example also shows the swing arm that was used to support the cooking pots and the firedogs beneath, which would have been used to raise the fire closer to the pots hanging above, when required.

A more traditionally-styled working kitchen fireplace, which incorporates some of the Colonial elements, can be seen in Adena, which is situated in Chillicothe, Ohio. Originally built in 1807 for Thomas Worthington, the Governor of Ohio, this beautiful Georgian house was restored relatively recently and it includes a typical early nineteenth century kitchen

fireplace. The mantel is shown used in the traditional way to hang utensils and cooking implements continually in use, and to store dishes. The open area of the chimney was made of the simplest brick, which was both very functional as well as giving some form of decoration to a practical piece.

As American Colonial style developed it became increasingly sophisticated, which was also mirrored in the fireplace design. Fine-quality items had been imported from England, but now they were increasingly made by local craftsmen—particularly in Boston. What distinguished Colonial from similar styles in England and Europe was very much the use of color. An example

Above: Harrison often used his house to conduct his official business. The kitchen chimneypiece shows a simple, and basic style; the form and function of this fireplace perfectly complement each other.

of this slightly later Colonial style is seen in Grouseland, the Vincennes, Indiana home of soon-to-be President William Henry Harrison. Built in 1804 after he was made Governor of Indiana, the house was often used by Harrison to conduct his official business, particularly the parlor, dining room and kitchen. The kitchen chimneypiece shows a simple, basic and efficient style, which epitomizes the later Colonial look. It incorporates a small range on which to cook, and the mantel is used only for storage of cooking pots and hanging utensils. The form and function of this fireplace perfectly compliment each other—it is a simple pleasure to both look at and sit beside. The Dining Room and the Parlor have much more of a flavor of English Georgian to them, although the vivid colors used on the walls are much more typical of the Colonial palette. The fireplaces, as befit rather more formal rooms, are of a simple Georgian-style design in paneled and white-painted wood, with a brick-lined fire opening. The walls of both these rooms are plain color, with no moldings or pattern, so the fireplace is a major feature of the room. Above each of them, rather than a mirror or overmantle, there is an oil painting in a simple gold frame.

Another and quite different Colonial style can be seen in the house of former President Franklin Pierce. The Pierce household, in Hillsboro, New Hampshire was completed in 1804, the year Franklin was born. Although their home was a typical wood-framed clapboard house, it was grand in scale and incorporated a ballroom. The inspiration for the interior design seems to have been partly from Scandinavia, with the chimneypiece in the master bedroom reflecting the simple wood paneling found in many Swedish homes today. The wide brick jambs and open fire area are completely without decoration, and only the fire dogs incorporate any design elements. The

Below: Grouseland, in Vincennes, the Indiana home of former President William Henry Harrison. Built in 1804, after he was made Governor of Indiana, the parlor was a favorite official meeting place.

actual chimney breast decoration consists simply of panel molding set acrossways in various widths, with the traditional gilt-framed family picture centered over the fireplace opening.

Like the master bedroom, the style of the kitchen fireplace in the Hillsboro house also reflects other influences. The rough-planed pine mantel and simple paneled overmantel again have a Scandinavian look, but this is combined with overtones that come from being designed and built in America.

The parlor fireplace has a more Georgian feel. The room is decorated with unusual pictorial wallpaper—brought home by Pierce from a trip to France—which is combined with plain wooden paneling below the dado to create the elegant design of this room. The classical lines of the fire surround again have no applied decoration, and reflect the simple style and feel that is very common in Colonial houses.

Stonewall, the ranch Lyndon B. Johnson bought from his aunt in 1951—and which served as the Texan White House during the Johnson administration—is a comfortably furnished house with a Colonial feel. One living room fireplace has a substantial chimney that reaches nearly to the ceiling—this should make the chimneypiece imposing, but instead it gives a homely feel to the room. One unusual element of this fireplace is the raised hearth, which is used as an extra seating area within the room and makes the whole chimneypiece feel like a part of the room. The scalloped edge to the canopy is another feature that is not usually seen on Colonial fireplaces—as they normally have very little or no decoration at all—but it looks quite natural on this chimney breast in the context of its setting. It is also functional as well as decorative, as it directs the smoke from the fire up to the chimney. The fireplace opening is lined with brick and stone—and it may have been used in earlier times for cooking, as the inner shelves have space to support pots and utensils on them.

The West Room in Stonewall has a

light and airy feel. The fireplace features a floor-to-ceiling stone chimney breast, with the plain wood mantel the only thing to break the sweep of the stone visually. Many Colonial-style fireplaces use simple and natural materials like this, with the only adornment being in natural wood—a simple wooden molding, for instance—or sometimes, as in the case of the West Room, the pattern formed by the key stones above the fire opening.

In the years immediately before the American Civil War, and for some time afterwards, architecture moved on and the Colonial style fell out of fashion as Gothic and Greek Revival ·became popular. However, tastes eventually came full circle—as they usually do—and today the American Colonial look is again desirable.

***Opposite:** The scalloped edge to the canopy of this fireplace, which is in the ranch of former President Lyndon B. Johnson, is quite unusual. Another uncommon element is the raised hearth that is used as seating.*

***Below:** The Classical lines of this fire surround in the parlor of the Pierce house reflect a simple style and feel very common in Colonial houses.*

Victorian Style

The Victorian period saw a wide variety of
fireplace styles, but it was still the
heart of the home.

Above: *Heavily carved dark oak was often used in Victorian fireplaces; it gives an
imposing feel to the parlor chimneypiece that is very typical of Victorian solidity.*

Opposite page: *Covering the mantel with a decorative cloth had begun to protect
Victorian sensibilities and modesty, but became a fashion.*

The nineteenth century was the time of the industrial revolution—an age of great change, which was reflected in the styles of architecture around at that time. This change of outlook was reflected clearly in the designs of houses—where previously the grace and elegance of Georgian and Regency houses prevailed, it became more and more obvious that, like the Victorian outlook on life, their houses were build in a solid and stoic manner. As many people did not own their houses, but merely rented them from large developers, the exterior architecture was generally designed and built all the same—inside was where people were able to impose their own taste and style and fashion was not always the first consideration. Traditions began to be broken, a new freedom came to the fore, and individual tastes began to show in the wide range of styles used. The fireplace became the center of social and family life—especially in the Parlor, the main room used for meeting guests and entertaining.

The early Victorian period saw a return of the romantic look, expressed in neo-Gothic and Elizabethan styles—often with rather regrettable consequences, as the taste for over-exaggeration was paramount. The far more elegant and stylish Greek revival showed a great deal more refinement in taste. Its austere classicism was at least restful on the eye; gone were the days of transforming the chimneypiece into a center of applied art. Instead of the ornate overmantle of previous years, a large mirror over a simple marble chimneypiece—often with Greek ornamentation, or the fashionable sphinx heads on pilasters supporting the overmantel—was used to great effect.

Sir John Soanes, the famous nineteenth-century architect, was a great exponent of this; he designed a new treatment for chimneypieces, which became exceedingly popular. By placing the frieze below the entablature and over the open mount, in line with the caps of the pilasters, the height of the fireplace was increased visually, without raising the height of the mantle shelf. It was still the fashion at the time to keep the mantles low, so that people could see themselves with ease in the mirror above. A prime example of this design can be seen in the Sir John Soane's House, now a museum in Lincoln's Inn Fields, in London, England.

Rather than the Regency aristocrat, the arbiter of taste was fast becoming the rich industrialist, and generally fireplace design—following interior design as a whole—lost all the Georgian harmony of the previous

Opposite page: The manufacture of cast iron surrounds and grates became so easy and cheap that they were suitable for the huge majority of houses being built in the rapidly growing industrial towns and cities.

Below: By placing the frieze below the entablature and over the open mount, in line with the caps of the pilasters, the height of the fireplace was increased visually. This was a common way to make a fireplace appear more imposing without increasing its height.

era. Strange and eclectic mixes of styles, often a very poor imitation of the originals, were commissioned by a rather less-than-discerning clientele. Medieval, Renaissance, Gothic and Naturalistic statues were seen in superfluous quantities—although there were many notable exceptions, which proved that at least some Victorians knew what was required to create an atmosphere of stately grandeur in a spectacular chimneypiece.

In the mid-nineteenth century, fireplaces became considerably more efficient as the innovations and designs of Count Rumford began to be implemented. First put forward in the late eighteenth century, they were finally adopted in the Victorian era. Count Rumford was an American, born plain Benjamin Thompson in Massachusetts. At nineteen, he married a rich New Hampshire spinster, several years older than himself. She in turn introduced him to the British colonial Governor—a John Wentworth, for whom he became a spy. Whilst serving as a soldier of fortune he was also pursuing his scientific research, which subsequently led to him being awarded a fellowship of

the Royal Society in London, England at the age of twenty-seven. His title of Count Rumford was awarded for re-organizing the Bavarian troops and ridding the countryside surrounding Munich of "tramps, beggars, vagrants, smugglers and defrauders of the customs, whom were put into the work house as cheap labor to make goods for the army." A series of essays were published by him in 1798, one of which was entitled "Of Chimney Fireplaces, with proposals for Improving them to save Fuel." This tackles the domestic fireplace, with ideas to make it more efficient and fuel-cost effective in use. Rumford had originally been researching the industrial application of the action of fire, but the London smog of that time persuaded him to look at its domestic use instead.

In the previous design of fireplaces, the width of the open chimney had been very large with the fire grate, back and side made from metal—usually cast iron. Although they looked very beautiful and elegant, these metal fire grates were, in fact, very inefficient. Adams fireplaces, made at the Carron works, were especially prone to the difficulties of an all-metal grate; when they were lit, the metal would absorb the heat and become very hot. Rumford showed that it was far better to use a material that was less heat-absorbent for the back and sides—this would then reflect the heat back into the room, and make the fire much more effective. Although he took some of his ideas from Benjamin Franklin, who himself had not been entirely original, he pushed his theories with energy, working in England to improve fireplaces and becoming a very rich man. When Rumford's ideas came into general use they also had implications on design. The smaller grate promoted by Rumford was often framed by an arched detailed opening, which was then surrounded by decorative ceramic tiles to create a very pretty effect. Fireplaces like this were mass-produced in their thousands in the later part of the nineteenth century, and became a forerunner to the Arts & Crafts designs, notably by Renée Mackintosh.

Left: This chimneypiece illustrates the different designs used by the late Victorians, which became a forerunner to the Arts & Crafts style.

Opposite page: The smaller grate promoted by Rumford was often framed by an arched detailed opening.

Taste was very unpredictable at this time, and just as Rumford's fireplace was being widely used a new trend was becoming apparent. The new fashion was for wider rectangular heaths, with log-burning fires. The logs would be lifted off the hearth with two large fire dogs or andirons, the designs of which underwent a revival with Shaw, Nestfield and Burges—the latter producing the most brilliant work in Cardiff Castle and his own house in Kensington, England. Being more suitable for large country houses, these wood burning chimneypieces were usually confined to the principal rooms, especially the large halls, while in the lesser rooms, such as the bedrooms, the more conventional fireplaces were used.

Another style popularized at that time was the high Gothic; probably the finest example of this can be seen at Knebworth House in the State Drawing Room. In 1843, when the author Bulwer-Lytton inherited the grand palace, the Gothic style was at its height and his aim became to turn it into a high Gothic Palace. One

architect, among many, who worked on the State Drawing Room was John Crace, who, together with Bulwer-Lytton, designed some of the hugely-decorated elaborate chimneypieces, the most magnificent at Knebworth. Their masterpiece consisted of a large overmantel mirror framed with niches containing figures—pinnacles of carved and gilded , red-gowned angel figurines, supporting a shield, stretching to the ceiling. The carved stonework of the arched hearth has a splendid marble Bittern in the center, which complements the same design incorporated in the firedogs. The Bittern is a bird that appears in the family crest of Lytton and it was repeated in decoration again and again at Knebworth. The tiles in the deep reveals either side were specially made for this chimneypiece, and also show the Bittern incorporated into their design, alongside the mottos and crests from all the

Below: *This Victorian fireplace, with its velvet drapes, is a typical example—it was as though anything naked offended their sense of decorum.*

Bulwer-Lytton families. There is also a family motto inscribed on the coving below the mantel shelf:

HOC VIRTUTIS OPUS (usual English translation: work of virtue)

As the Victoria reign progressed, the design of fireplaces became even more varied in their styles. A burst of mock-Tudor architecture around 1870 resulted in a taste for twisted chimneys and huge stone hearths becoming fashionable. It also brought back a semblance of the great oak chimneypieces of that period, but with a Victorian slant. A wide mantelshelf supported on brackets above the fire opening consisted of a series of balusters and little balustrades, often turned in a candy twist design. These would partition off the shelf into compartments, for knick-knacks and

Above: *A very simple Victorian style fireplace—the tiled surround is of interest as it is reflected in the matching tiles of the hearth. This was not usual, as the delicate nature of the tiles made them susceptible to damage.*

other ornaments typical of the Victorian age. The Victorians had a passion for covering everything, as though anything naked offended their sense of decorum; this was shown in a multitude of ways including the fashion for fireplace decoration. The general method was to fix a large board on top of the wood or cast iron mantelshelf, a piece of cloth made of serge or velvet would then be draped from this. The fringe was often bobbled and would, of course, attract dust and dirt from the fire at an alarming rate. Together with the multitude of ornaments also present on the overmantel, it was no surprise that the Victorians employed live in or daily help. Splendid examples of the Victorian style can be seen in places such as the Lockwood-Mathews Mansion in Norwalk, Connecticut, which is open to the public and features many interesting chimneypieces.

In the latter part of Victoria's reign, one of the most influential designers was William Morris; his revival of the inglenook fireplace followed a trend for the individualistic style. His feeling was that mass-produced, machine-made articles had destroyed the soul of the artist. Morris would work on every detail of the chimneypieces he designed— they were beautifully thought out, with all the different materials used working in complete harmony and bringing to the fore all the craftsmans' skills available to him. From decorative ceramic tiles, woodcarving and metal work, Morris progressed his designs and ideas into weaving, mural painting and wallpaper printing. The range of materials available to him, and the scope of his ideas, influenced architects and designers for many years; what had initially seemed to be over-fussy and too detailed, Morris formed into a feeling of coherent taste, homeliness and cozy charm.

The architect M.H. Baillie Scott who described the average cast iron fireplace as "painfully ugly" also championed the inglenook fireplace. His thoughts on the inglenook were that, with its broad brick hearth, wide settle, and rough hewn oak beams, a simple home dignity of style should be the aim, and the tendency to over-ornamentation prevalent at the time should be ignored. His preference for the use of brickwork instead of the glazed tile, which he felt was too hard, and his regard for the hearth to be a symbol of home life encouraged his desire to incorporate the inglenook fireplace into small rooms. The idea of offsetting the chimneypiece in an asymmetrical fashion to the room, incorporating one of the walls and allowing the placement of a long seat or settle—to be situated so as not to cut off the fireplace from the rest of the room— was indeed a sensible option. The placement of the fixed seating he regarded as paramount—it should be placed the right distance from the fire and proportioned for maximum comfort.

As in previous ages, the fireplace was a faithful reflection of a way of life; the family meeting place. As an indication of social progress, this was never truer than in the Victorian era. In the world at large, so much was happening so quickly, with the eighties and the nineties being decades of intense artistic re-evaluation. The production of manufactured goods was on a scale never seen before and while some designers took the view of Oscar Wilde that "All machinery may be beautiful, even when it is undecorated," others were of the view that to "revive artistic craftsmanship was paramount." The manufacture of cast iron surrounds and grates became so easy and cheap that they were very suitable for the many houses being built in the rapidly growing industrial towns and cities.

In America, a great number of houses were built for industrialists at this time, who, because of their thriving businesses, were able to afford have things built to their own designs. Since Victorian style was all the rage, many examples of it exist today. In a vast number of fireplaces the all-iron surround replaced the carved marble

chimneypiece from the eighteenth century, cast in such a way as to reflect the traditional classical composition of the earlier pieces. This fashion soon passed, and was replaced by a trend towards decorative ceramic tiles. These had been used previously just as a border for the fire, but they now began to form part of the whole chimneypiece, the design being based on unadorned simplicity for the surround, with the decoration coming from the tiles themselves. A perfect example of this can be seen in Wightwick Castle, where William Morris demonstrated his love of nature with the heavily flower-patterned tiles and the austere wood surround of the chimneypiece as a whole. As the world moved into the twentieth century, natural forms and designs came to be regarded as the height of contemporary fashion.

Below: *An elegant overmantel, which shows the Victorians' disposition to cover every available space with ornaments. The fireplace itself has the typical cast iron center with decorative tiles on either side.*

Modernist Style

The Modernist style ranges from the clean
lines of Art Deco, through the flamboyance
of Art Nouveau.

Above: In this chimneypiece, designed by William Morris, the extra wide opening
accomodate settles on either side that are are complemented by the oak paneling.

Left: The fireplace in the Grand Hall of Wingspread, designed by Frank Lloyd
Wright. The central chimneypiece rises the full height and dominates the space,.

With the advent of the new century a new fashion for pared down elegance arrived. Rennie Mackintosh was the best-known architect of this style—after the excesses of the Victorians and their over-cluttered designs, Mackintosh's simple Arts & Crafts elegance was an enormous change. With his style of architecture, it brought together a total concept in interior and architectural design, something which

Above: Art Nouveau was a conscious and clear attempt to move into a more fluid style—a move away from structure into more organic forms.

had been sadly lacking in the last century. In 1893 Mackintosh revealed his great debt to the architect and designer W.R. Lethaby, whose ideas and theories were published in the book Architecture, Mysticism and Myth the previous year. In expressing his views to fellow architects, he called on them to abandon their self-conscious use of antiquated details and to "go back to nature." He advised them to "clothe modern ideas with modern dress," a bold statement against the eclecticism that had gone before—and not designed to enamor him to the more established architects of the day. However, from an early age he had been taught by his farther, who was a keen gardener, to respect nature, and in its various forms, textures and colors it was to provide him with an invaluable source of inspiration. In designing the fireplaces for his spectacular rooms, Mackintosh never let the design overpower the interior, even though the sheer scale of some of them would seem to dominate the space. He is renowned for his great white mantel pieces—most were seven feet long and empty of any elaborate carving, the interest being created with the play of light reflecting upon the pigeonholes. Future designs followed this theme, often with simple hob grates, and occasionally with colored glass mosaics or inset ceramic tiles.

A rare example of his skill in adornment, while still keeping the simplicity he required, is in the fire surround in the drawing room at Hill House. Here he promotes the use of mosaics, incorporating his unique

designs into the pattern, which is unmistakably Mackintosh, and adorning the fireplace with fire irons made to his specific designs. He thus creates a unique whole, completed by a gesso panel made by his wife Margaret Macdonald, which hung above and complimented his style perfectly. His love of nature and naturalistic design marked his work as very avant-garde, with influences from Japanese art. As it began to evolve, it moved on from the pure and simple lines of his early years to the more Art Nouveau designs he produced later.

In contrast to the austere and simple lines of the Arts & Crafts movement, Art Nouveau was a conscious and clear attempt to move into a style independent of tradition—a precise move away from structure into the more organic. Items of wood and metal were contorted into undulating lines, the structures seemed to grow from their source. This nature-inspired, essentially curvilinear and asymmetric style, originated on the continent in the late nineteenth century, with Paris and

Below: *The Arts & Crafts style was epitomized by Wiliam Morris. His ability to design all the elements of a room—including the furniture and fabric—made his ideas come together in a unique way.*

Opposite page: Hollyhock House in California, designed in 1917 by Frank Lloyd Wright for Aline Barnsdale, was decorated with highly abstract and geometric motifs taken from Mayan art. In the living room, above the rather futuristic fireplace, stands a stylized carved overmantel panel that depicts the owner, his client, as an enthroned Indian queen surveying her desert kingdom.

Brussels being the major places of origin. It was not seen in Britain until a few years later, with Mackintosh being one of the main exponents. He also became very popular abroad and his work was much admired—although he carried out only one or two private commissions. The fireplaces of this period were often made with a cast iron surround polished to resemble pewter, and incorporating flowers, especially lilies, into the design. The lines of the mantel shelf were often curved and flowed along the top of the chimneypiece in a fluid movement. Tiles were sometimes used to decorate the sides, and as the vogue for stylized women was at its height, often a group of tiles, depicted a ethereal figure surrounded by organic shapes, would be used in a asymmetric fashion around the fire opening.

Art Deco can be said to have been influenced from many directions, not least the Arts & Crafts movement. This came about in a surprising way, with the early American exponents later inspiring designers such as Frank Lloyd Wright. His creations later in his life were streamlined and similar to the Bauhaus style, but for the majority of his career, he faithfully followed an Arts & Crafts design aesthetic. At its height in 1925, Art Deco was seen around the world, the Paris Exposition leading the way for many designers to follow. It became one of the styles that transcended countries and influenced designers worldwide, and it is still produced today. From the Chrysler building in New York to the Main Post Office in Kansas City, nearly every major city in the U.S.A. possessed some influence of Deco design—or "le style 25" as it was known then.

The angular lines and rectilinear feel to chimneypieces produced at this time made them significantly different to the fluidity of the Nouveau style. Elegance and opulence began to be seen again in the Deco period; French interiors reflected the fashion for "style." Fireplaces following this trend became a feature, which—although still integrated into the whole design of the room—stood apart as a piece on its own. Often

constructed entirely of mirrors, the fire surround would stand unadorned in the space. Very little would be put upon the mantel shelf, which was set low to follow the linear feel of the rest of the room. Perhaps a clock or a Renee Lalique piece of glass might be placed on top, but the look would always be uncluttered and clean. Enamels and tiles were sometimes used on the cheeks of the chimneypiece, to bring a little more color into the design.

Following the voracious appetite for other cultures that was linked to Art Deco, two which came to the fore were the indigenous American Aztecs and Mayans. By far the biggest influence on architecture and design in this area was Frank Lloyd Wright. The Hollyhock House he designed for Aline Barnsdale in 1917 in California was decorated with motifs taken from highly abstract and geometric Mayan art. In the living room, above the futuristic fireplace, stands a stylized overmantel panel depicting the owner, his client, as an enthroned Indian queen surveying her desert kingdom. This fireplace stands in the center of the room, dominating the space with its decorative overmantel and projecting hearth. It is surrounded by a pool of water, thus bringing a part of the outdoors inside. What also distinguishes this innovative design are the materials used in its construction. Whereas previously bricks, wood, metal or marble were the main components in the manufacture of fireplaces, Frank Lloyd Wright was a great experimentalist and loved to try different materials. Hollyhock House was a perfect example of the use of unusual materials exploited for architectural use. His innovative design was created in hollow clay tiles covered in stucco—this had the advantage of being light in structure, but giving the impression of great weight. Combined with its simple chiseled design, the most overriding impression of this fireplace is that it is a piece of monolithic propositions.

The Ennis House—also built in California, in 1923—was another unusual Wright design that was finally constructed after many problems with the concrete blocks used as the construction material. It has some unique features, which Wright did not use again in his designs. The chimneypiece in the main room is very simple in design, with the ornamentation coming from the molded concrete squares. Above the mantel can be seen one of the last remaining glass

Above: The Ennis House, built in 1923 in California. Above the mantel can be seen one of the last remaining glass mosaics designed by Wright. The form shows how nature and organic shapes influenced his ideas.

Opposite page: Wingspread, in Wisconsin, was designed in 1937, and was one of the last "prairie" style houses to be completed. The main chimneypiece is situated centrally in the Great Hall.

mosaics designed by Wright. The form shows how nature and organic forms influenced his ideas, a concept used previously in the Arts & Craft styled pieces but which Wright incorporated into his Mayan influenced architecture with ease.

A similar project to Hollyhock House in design and implementation was the one Wright designed for his friend John Sowden. Built in 1926, it was quite unique in its architectural concept. Entered from below, between copper gates in a stylized leaf and water design, the guest would be lead through dark corridors to reach the inner sanctum. This was the central core of the house, around which the rest of it was built. It used the concept of steel-reinforced concrete blocks, the designs of which reflected the Aztec Indian influence predominant in Wright's work at the time. One of the rooms, which leads off from the inner courtyard, was the living room; the fireplace dominated this space. Huge in proportion, it stood like an altar, carved with ancient forms, and it was both beautiful and immense in style. The firedogs, which stand in front, are replacements for the originals, which had a very Deco flavor with their clear linear look that was a familiar part of Deco design. Either side of the fireplace, and integral to it, are stools that originally had circular cushions, a concept going back to earlier centuries, when seats were placed as part of the chimneypiece.

Wingspread, in Wisconsin, was designed in 1937, and was one of the last "prairie" style houses to be completed. The main chimneypiece is central to the Great Hall, and instead of concrete blocks Wright used warm red bricks, not only for the fireplace but also for most of the internal architecture. The main house consists of four wings in a pinwheel layout leading off the central Great Hall, and the dramatic chimney dominates the space. Four fireplaces are situated on this chimney at the lower levels, giving a more intimate feel to the spaces surrounding them. Another unusual feature of Wingspread was the use of a mezzanine floor. This also had a fireplace utilizing the same central chimney, but on a higher level. Wright's innovative fire grates, which he designed individually to suit each separate fireplace, were often detailed to the extreme. In the case of Wingspread, each fire grate was shaped into a circular design with concentric bars, and stood out from the fire some considerable distance. Every fireplace had its own individual style, whilst still being part of the whole overall design. The brickwork in the architecture and design of the chimney and each separate fireplace is considered the finest of all Wright's work.

Left: *Taliesin West is building constructed in "desert rubblestone," in which the natural desert stones were cast in concrete. The fireplace in the living room has such an organic quality that it seems to grow out of the desert itself. Its distinct style has evolved and been dictated by the natural elements of the materials used.*

The Evans House, built in California in 1936, was a reflection of the style of Deco architecture now becoming predominant in the U.S.A. The building covered only two stories and, like most of Wright's architecture, was unusual in its floor arrangement. His choice of natural materials, such as a cedar shingle roof, and cypress wood doors and paneling, gave this building a very clean uncluttered feel and this is reflected inside by the minimalist lines. The fireplace in the living room is also very minimalist in design, consisting of a beautiful patinated copper panel, sitting unadorned in the center of the mantel. The brickwork either side, the only detailed item on the chimney, has plain cypress panels on either side. This was one of the plainest and most stylish of Wright's fireplace designs.

Taliesin West, begun in Arizona in 1937 and added to until 1959, is a desert rubblestone construction, in which natural desert stones were cast in concrete. In Taliesin the living room fireplace is the most interesting piece. It has a very organic quality and seems to literally grow out of the wall. The rugged stone facade of the chimney breast reflects the Sonoran Desert in which it was built. Flanked by giant pieces of red wood, the fireplace has a distinct style of its own, which has evolved and been dictated by the natural movement and form of the materials used.

The Zimmerman House, built in 1950 in New Hampshire, was one of Wright's Usonian houses. These were developed around the time of the Second World War as a solution to the small economical house and as Wright's response to the modern architecture being produced by Corbusier. He continued to produce his Usonian house well after the end of the war, as they had become very popular. The brickwork of the Zimmerman House takes on a very regimented style and the plain surface of the bricks themselves is used as a decorative feature. The asymmetrical fireplace in the living room rises right up into the gable of the roof and divides the open-plan living area into two halves. The materials of the fireplace, brick and stone, neatly repeat and echo the materials used on the exterior. The design of the interior is very clean and modernistic, and the fireplace fits in with this theme. The simple, horizontal lines of the stone lintels are offset by the changing levels of the vertical surfaces, to create a pleasing rhythm. The fire grate is a plain construction of iron bars, built into the brickwork and large enough to hold a roaring log fire.

The Loveness House in Minnesota is one of the very last of the Usonian houses, having been built in 1955. The main material used for its construction was a local limestone, known as Dolomite, which is also used extensively in the interior. The fireplace, which almost fills one wall of the main room, is a massive construction of natural-surfaced limestone blocks, with the fireplace opening offset to one side of the chimney breast. The hearth is of the same pale stone, set into the red, ceramic tiles of the floor. The fire grate is a simple grid of iron bars, set off the ground on short legs, and big enough to hold several large logs. Harking back to the designs of much earlier days is the small built-in stone bench to one side of the fire, with its inviting and comfortable cushions.

After such a strong period of development, which had led to so many unique styles and trends at the beginning of the twentieth century, it seems strange that apathy for fireplace design then set in. A possible reason for this could be advent of the Second World War—but this did not stop the work still being designed and constructed by Wright. The main reason is probably that the movement of taste from traditional to the minimalist style of living, and the economics of heating the home with fuels that were rapidly becoming short in supply, influenced people into new ways of thinking.

Below: *The Loveness House in Minnesota. The fireplace, which almost fills one wall of the main room, is a massive construction of natural-surfaced limestone blocks.*

Opposite page: *The Zimmerman house interior is very clean and modernistic, and the fireplace fits this theme. The simple, horizontal lines of the stone lintels are offset by the changing levels of the vertical surfaces.*

Contemporary Style

Technical innovation and new materials take fireplace design into the future.

Above: *Now fires do not need visual fuel to burn, the flames can appear from unusual sources, such as this "firebowl."*

Opposite page: *A very modern take on the traditional theme of a kitchen chimneypiece—a wood-burning fireplace place high within the wall itself.*

In the last half of the twentieth century, the fireplace entered a rather stagnant period of design with very little innovation. With the end of the Second World War and the rise in commercially-built houses, the fireplace seemed to lose its place in the home. So many houses were built in this period with no central focus for the rooms—historically that had always been one of the functions of the fireplace. However, with the new fashion for economical and functional ways of heating the home, it became unusual to have a fireplace at all, and only very grand houses retained the style and elegance of the previous century. Also rejected were those designs that were deemed to be unpractical and labor intensive in use, as it was now no longer common to have extra domestic help in the home.

Many of the original fireplaces in old buildings had been removed in the early part of the twentieth century—along with other period features—in the quest for a more "modern" look. However, towards the end of the century many people were looking back nostalgically to a previous era, and they wanted to recreate the homely and secure feel that they imagined for those days in their homes. The reproduction of traditional-style fireplaces became a growth industry, feeding this demand to replace "original" features. For a very long time the fireplace industry was led by the manufacturers, and had no strong design input at all, despite the creative activity that was occurring elsewhere in the interior design world.

However, now modern architecture has come into its own and the design of fireplaces has begun to catch up—and what has evolved over subsequent years are designs that are both beautiful, unusual and time-saving. Often—because of the unusual and innovative materials used in them—these fireplaces also create a new focal point for the rooms in which they stand, thus bringing them vividly to life. The intense feeling of personal security that an open fire projects—with its leaping flames and warm, cosy light—can never be replaced or reproduced within sterile rooms with artificial forms of heating.

Right: *Now modern architecture has come into its own, fireplaces can create a new focal point for the rooms in which they stand, thus bringing them to life. The intense feeling of personal security that an open fire projects can never be replaced or reproduced.*

New homes are now designed to suit every particular taste—whichever century that may be. Some stunning new homes look ultra modern, others ostensibly date back hundreds of years but in reality are brand new, so people have a choice of exactly what style or feel they would like. This has given architects and designers an unprecedented ability to expand the form and range of fireplace designs—and now there are people who only design fireplaces, rather than leaving them to the architect designing the rest of the building. These designers have such a vast scope for producing new and unusual designs, which are both cost effective and environmentally clean, that the possibilities for the fireplace have become boundless. The return of the fireplace to fashion also means that even modernistic buildings of today can still be warm and welcoming homes—and that there is a fireplace style that will fit them without clashing.

Opposite page: *The origin of this modernistic design dates back to Saxon times, when the fire was placed in a hole in the wall. This has evolved into the clean modern lines popular today.*

Below: *The use of natural materials—such as metal, stone and glass—in modern fireplaces has also become very popular, particularly when they are featured in new and eye-catching ways.*

In some isolated areas, the unavailability of utilities such as gas or electricity means that wood- or coal-burning fireplaces are still in use. But as people became more environmentally friendly and it was realized that the natural sources of energy we had so often taken for granted were become short in supply, it became imperative that modern fireplace designers came up with practical solutions to the problems presented. There is now so much technology at hand that the scope is endless for the type of energy that can be used for heating, which has also had a great influence on the design of fireplaces.

Some designs have, in fact, come almost full circle, to approach the Saxon concept of a hole in the wall and a central hearth. Part of what has made this change possible is again the advance in technology, which now enables smoke to be mechanically extracted to outside walls. This means the smoke can be removed quickly and efficiently from the fireplace straight to the exterior, which negates the requirement for a chimney or flue. Flues can also now be run under the floorboards, or concealed inside walls or other structural features, so fireplaces can really be situated almost anywhere within a room.

More and more people are taking an interest in the design of their home and, with the constraints on what is fashionable or correct having been removed, designers such as Carolyn and Christian Outersterp of CVO began to tackle the fireplace for the general market. Taking full advantage of the noticeable and widespread innovations that have appeared since the start of the twenty-first century, they have taken the design and technology of the fireplace to new heights. Carolyn started in business fifteen years ago, producing fireplaces with her brothers when the industry was dominated by "men in suits." She then moved on and set up CVO in 1999, to answer the needs of a public short-changed by years of indifference. She is one of the only women in the industry—although that may be changing, as she and her contemporaries are bringing glamour and detail back into a subject that had somehow lost its way.

Nowadays 90% of new fireplaces are installed to take gas fires, which brings attendant problems of its own. Each new fireplace concept has to be run through a rigorous series of testing procedures, to make sure

that it can pass the extremely strict regulations now covering gas fires. These tests cost the manufacturer between £10,000–20,000 and any subsequent alteration to the design, size or shape—however small—ensures that the fireplace model will have to run through all of these tests again at a similar cost. This expense has to be passed onto the public to a certain extent, but as awareness increases in the marketplace mass production will bring the costs down—as in any cutting edge product. But for most architects and designers to whom style and design are paramount, cost is a secondary issue. Often the most unusual and unique designs are required for public buildings, hotels or very large private homes.

The use of natural materials in fireplaces has also become very popular recently, with the most unusual elements being used for the fire itself. Instead of the traditional look of a fire with coal or wood, now it is common to see pebbles or metal in strange shapes, from which the flames appear. Another interesting point is that now people are less and less interested in the heat emitted by the fireplace, and are merely

looking for the "flame picture" without the heat. This can be very difficult to achieve, as technology has not yet come up with a method of extracting the heat from flames! Perhaps this is the next step for the second half of the twenty-first century?

Fireplaces will never entirely lose their place within the home—as we have seen over the centuries, the feeling of warmth and welcome, and the ability to make an often imposing house into a living and breathing home, can never be underestimated. Deep within us we all have the desire to settle with our loved ones in front of the fireside.

Left: *In these days of centrally-heated homes, fireplaces no longer need to provide heat or light—so they also do not need a visual form of fuel to burn. The attraction of this unusual modern fireplace is the eye-catching way the flame seemingly appears from nowhere.*

Below: *The sources of fire in today's fireplaces can often be from very unusual and unexpected items—such as the "fire-vessel," or bowl, shown here set into an opening in the wall. This has opened up a wide variety of new options to suit almost every taste and accommodate every kind of modern home.*

Picture Credits